daily insights

Leadership
matters

to inspire extraordinary results

Lee J. Colan, Ph.D.

Leadership
matters

daily insights to inspire extraordinary results

Inquiries regarding permission for use of the material contained in this book should be addressed to:

CornerStone Leadership Institute
P.O. Box 764087
Dallas, TX 75376
888.789.5323

Printed in the United States of America
ISBN: 978-0-9819242-9-8

Credits

Copy Editor	Juli Baldwin, The Baldwin Group, Dallas, TX Juli@BaldwinGrp.com
Proofreader	Kathleen Green, Positively Proofed, Plano, TX positivelyproofed@sbcglobal.net
Design, art direction & production	Melissa Monogue, Back Porch Creative, Plano, TX info@BackPorchCreative.com

Contents

Leadership Matters

• • ● • •

At the beginning of the day, it's all about possibilities. At the end of the day, it's all about results. But in today's ultra-competitive marketplace, good results aren't good enough. To win, you need to produce extraordinary results. Extraordinary results come from extraordinarily performing teams. And where there is an extraordinary team, you can bet there is an inspiring leader. That's why leadership – specifically, *your* leadership – matters.

Leadership matters because extraordinarily performing teams are the ultimate advantage for any organization – a business, a non-profit, a sports team, or a family for that matter. New or unique products or services might get you into the game, but only your team can deliver victory and create a "wall" that is higher and harder for your competitors to climb.

Leadership matters … right now, today … no matter what situation you find yourself in. Whether you lead a team of one or a team of 100, leadership matters. Whether you lead at home, at the office, in one city or across the globe, leadership matters. It matters when you are on the front lines of an organization and as you work your way up to the very top. It matters in an up economy or a down economy, in a start-up or a mature business, in local business or a global enterprise.

Inspiring leadership is the single biggest factor in achieving extraordinary results. It might be hard to believe that one factor can have such a profound impact on performance, but our daily experiences – as well as plenty of research – prove it over and over again. A recent study of 30,000 leaders found that the top 10 percent of leaders generated twice the net income as the middle 80 percent. The study also identified one critical competency that distinguished the top 10th percentile of leaders from the rest: the ability to inspire and motivate others to high performance. These findings demonstrate that inspiring leadership is directly linked with both employee engagement and productivity. In fact, the researchers stated, "… in addition to the responsibilities outlined in their job descriptions, [leaders] need to inspire and motivate people if the company is to succeed."[1]

This book presents 31 matters of leadership. The topics are presented in a rapid-read, daily format designed for today's information-rich, time-poor world. For easy reference, they are organized in alphabetical order.

At the end of each daily topic, you will find brief questions to help you bridge the gap between insight and application. There is great power in converting your thoughts into words, so be sure to write down your responses to each question. Then, turn your words into action that same day. To support your action, you can access free tools – just scan the QR codes at the end of selected chapters or visit theLgroup.com/LeadershipMatters.

Leadership Matters was written to inspire you to elevate your leadership so that you, in turn, can inspire your team. Imagine the possibilities if your team could consistently achieve extraordinary results …

   ○ What would it mean for your organization?

   ○ What would it mean for your team?

   ○ What would it mean for you and your career?

[1] *How Extraordinary Leaders Double Profits*, Jack Zenger, Joe Folkman and Scott Edinger, 2010

Let's get started and find out. Your team is depending on you ... because your leadership matters!

"Everything rises and falls on leadership. Leadership is the difference maker and the deal breaker. It's how we grow organizations. It's how we impact lives. But leadership cannot be an idea we simply talk about. Leadership is the action we must live out."

– JOHN MAXWELL

Appreciation

● ● ● ● ●

William James, the father of psychology, stated that the most fundamental psychological need is to be appreciated. We all want to feel fully appreciated for our work. The payoff for inspiring leaders is that **people do more for those who appreciate them.**

Although leaders widely recognize the need for appreciation, it tends to be a blind spot. That is, we generally believe we are much more appreciative of our team than our team thinks we are. For example, I think I am more appreciative of my wife than she feels appreciated by me. The same can be said of most leaders and team members. The reason is that we often do not convert our invisible thoughts of appreciation into visible acts of appreciation.

With all of today's technology options, it's easy to find ourselves too busy for face-to-face interaction, but that's one of the best ways to charge up our teams. **Showing appreciation is not a matter of time and intention; rather, it's a matter of priority and action.**

Research by former Gallup chairman, the late Donald Clifton, revealed that workgroups with at least a 3-to-1 ratio of positive to negative interactions were significantly more productive than those having less than a 3-to-1 ratio. In other words, more productive teams had at least three positive interactions for every one negative interaction. By the way, the same study showed the bar was set even higher for more successful marriages – the key ratio was 5-to-1. Showing your appreciation is certainly a positive interaction and is a simple way to boost your ratio.

Consider tracking your ratio for a week to gauge how well you are appreciating your team. Look for opportunities to **acknowledge your team's results *and* positive progress.** This is basic psychology – reinforce those behaviors that you want to see more frequently. Catch them doing something right … and do it often. If you look for your team doing something right, opportunities to reinforce them will be plentiful. The key is to be sincere and specific. In other words, don't fall into the trap of blurting out the robotic "Good job". Take the time to thoughtfully explain why you appreciated the specific action taken by a team member. For example, you might say, "Kayla, I really appreciate the way you quickly resolved that customer issue without adding more time or cost to our delivery schedule. That makes a big difference for the company."

Demonstrating appreciation for your team and their efforts can put them on the fast track to inspired performance. There should be plenty of opportunities since a Harris poll found that **65 percent of the workers reported receiving *no recognition* for good work in the past year!** That's a pretty low bar. So, we should not worry about recognizing our teams too much. In fact, there are no documented studies of any team ever feeling over-appreciated.

Here are some simple ways to make recognition a defining moment for your team:

- ○ Say "Thank You!" – An all-too-obvious, yet highly underused, form of appreciation.

- ○ Go old school and write a card or note to a team member expressing why you appreciate him or her.

○ Allow your team to present their work to your boss. This is a great way to engage your team, and it also shows your boss what kind of leader you are.

○ Offer team members a choice of projects on which to work. When team members buy into a project, they will put their hearts into it.

○ Put a sincere acknowledgement in your company or department newsletter. This takes only a few minutes of your time but creates long-term "trophy value" for the employee.

○ Tell an employee's story of accomplishment at a staff meeting. Detailed stories are perceived as more interesting, meaningful, thoughtful and memorable.

○ Take a team member to lunch to show your appreciation. Remember to do more listening than talking.

Find ways that are natural and comfortable for you to demonstrate your appreciation since **your authenticity is the key.** The good news is that we have complete control over our appreciation. No budget limitations or excuses here – there are literally thousands of ways to demonstrate our appreciation at little or no cost.

What is the positive-to-negative ratio on my team?

_____

_____

_____

What one thought of appreciation can I convert into a
tangible act of appreciation today?

_____

_____

_____

"There is more hunger for
    love and appreciation
        in this world than for bread."

– MOTHER TERESA

Attention

● ● ● ● ●

Time is a great equalizer; it runs at the same speed for everybody, rich or poor, jet pilot or snail farmer. You can't manufacture time, you can't reproduce time, you can't slow time down or turn it around and make it run in the other direction. As the saying goes, "life is like a roll of toilet paper. The closer you get to the end, the faster is goes."

We cannot really manage time, but we can manage our attention. Attention is a resource we all possess. Your attention reflects your conscious decisions about which activities will occupy your time. You are where your attention is … not necessarily where your body is. Whereas **time is the great equalizer, attention is the great differentiator.**

Once we are made aware of something in our environment, if we pay attention to it, we will see more of it. For example, when was the last time you saw a yellow car? Maybe yesterday or last week? Now, if you live in New York City, you see hundreds of yellow taxis daily. Even still, you can look for yellow cars that are not taxis.

Now that I have made you aware of yellow cars, you will start seeing more yellow cars in the following days. Has there been a sudden invasion of bright yellow cars? Of course not. They've been there all along. The difference is, now you are aware of them – you have a heightened awareness of yellow cars. I call this connection between heightened awareness and more frequent sightings *The Yellow Car Phenomenon.*

The first time I became aware of *The Yellow Car Phenomenon* was when my wife was pregnant with our first child. We spent our weekends driving from store to store shopping for all that wonderful baby stuff. Then at lunch at work the next week, I looked around and thought to myself, "Oh my goodness, there must be something in the water here in Dallas. Everyone is pregnant!" No doubt, I had breezed by hundreds of expectant mothers before, never paying much attention. Now that my wife was pregnant, it seemed that everyone else was also. Amazing!

It's the power of personal attention. If your mind is ready to pay attention to something – new people you want to meet, selling opportunities, new applications for an old product, ways to save money, new markets to enter, chances to learn a new skill, ways to generate more income – you will start seeing more of it. These things have always been there, but now you're paying attention to them. **When you change the way you look at things, things change the way they look.**

Instead of paying attention to every single piece of information in our stimulus-rich world, if we really look for those things we want in our team, business or family, that's exactly what we will find. Keeping the *Yellow Car Phenomenon* in mind, if we pay attention to the positive, we see positive. For example:

Look for...	See...
○ Humor	○ Life as comedy
○ Signs of positive progress	○ Good performance to recognize
○ Cooperation	○ Teamwork
○ Opportunities to coach	○ Coachable moments

On the other hand, if we look for negative things, that's what we will see more of:

Look for...	See...
○ Drama	○ Dysfunctional team
○ Mistakes	○ Underperformers and frustration
○ Hidden agendas	○ Selfish behavior

It's the power of our attention. For proof, just count how many yellow cars you notice tomorrow.

Where do I tend to focus my attention during the day?

_____

_____

_____

Where do I need to focus my attention in order to inspire myself? My team? My family?

_____

_____

_____

What "yellow car" am I paying attention to this week?

_____

_____

_____

"You can become blind by seeing each day as a similar one. Each day is a different one, each day brings a miracle of its own. It's just a matter of paying attention to this miracle."

– PAULO COELHO

Attitude

Inspiring leadership is defined by an inspiring attitude. **Inspiring words and acts are preceded by an inspiring attitude.** Like it or not, our thoughts and interpretations of people and circumstances directly influence our beliefs, and ultimately, our leadership actions.

Yes, bad things do happen and they sometimes "just show up." Any leader would be hard pressed to remember a week when no curve balls were thrown at him or her. However, it is our interpretation that makes a situation negative. A surprise event or a challenging moment doesn't have to drag us down. The way we choose to think about what happens determines the ultimate outcome. Henry Ford once said, "Whether you think you can or cannot, you're right." In other words, your attitude reflects your past, describes your present and predicts your future.

Our experiences are much less important than our attitude toward them. Our interpretations of experiences either limit or enable our future success. Here's an example: A mission-critical project you are leading has "promotion" written all over it, but it bombs – it's over budget, past its deadline ... the works. How you choose to interpret those facts is how you shape your future. Do you see yourself as a failure, a poor leader who is maxed out and on the way out? Or are you a great leader in the making who is learning some tough lessons that will help ensure success on the next project?

Think the best ALL the time. What's the harm? If you choose to protect yourself from disappointment by always thinking the worst, you have also chosen disappointment as the filter through which you view all things and people ... and that's just what you will get. On the other hand, you can choose to think the best all the time. Sure, you might be disappointed occasionally but, most of the time, you will be programming your mental attitude to achieve your best. This creates a tremendously powerful chain reaction that looks like:

You think the best of your team

Team performs to meet you expectations

Customers' expectations are met

Better business results

You think the best because you have seen the
benefit of doing so.

We must manage our attitude as carefully as we manage
our money. At any moment during daily leadership, we
can fall victim to our own attitude. Self-doubt and fear
are the enemies of inspired leadership. Instead, choose an
attitude of victory and your team's performance will follow.

What does my attitude today say about the results I can expect tomorrow?

_____

_____

_____

How does my attitude toward my own capabilities, my team and my goals affect my leadership?

_____

_____

_____

 Take a free *Attitude Tune-up* and receive a real-time feedback report.
theLgroup.com/LeadershipMatters

"There's very little difference in people. But that little difference makes a big difference. The little difference is attitude. The BIG DIFFERENCE is whether it is positive or negative."

– W. CLEMENT STONE

Coaching

At one time, Andrew Carnegie was the wealthiest man in America. He came to America from his native Scotland when he was a small boy, did a variety of odd jobs, and eventually ended up as the largest steel manufacturer in the United States. At one time, he had 43 millionaires working for him. In those days, a millionaire was a rare person.

A reporter asked Carnegie how he had hired 43 millionaires. Carnegie responded that those men had not been millionaires when they started working for him but had become millionaires as a result.

The reporter's next question was, "How did you develop these men to become so valuable to you that you have paid them this much money?" Carnegie replied that men are developed the same way gold is mined. When gold is mined, several tons of dirt must be moved to get an ounce of gold, but one doesn't go into the mine looking for dirt – one goes in looking for the gold.

Some leaders find themselves sitting on a mountain of gold, and yet they feel poor because they don't know how to mine the gold from their teams. Coaching is how we mine our team's gold.

Inspiring leaders coach good team members to become better people. They help them build better lives for themselves and others. They build their team from the inside out … inspiring excellence at work and in life.

In the crunch of daily demands, we sometimes forget a fundamental law of leadership: If our teams are successful, we are successful. Inspiring leaders are crystal clear on this law and focus on nurturing success and inspiring future leaders.

The coaching challenge in today's mega-busy workplace is that people only remember 20 percent of what they hear.

And if those people are teenagers, you can divide that number in half!

Why is this percentage so low? Let's say I am hurried and swing by a team member's cube and say, "Ryan, please make sure you use the new format on the month-end sales report … thanks." Even if Ryan is a pretty sharp guy, what do you think the chances are he will hear my request accurately, remember it, recall it accurately when it's relevant, interpret my instructions as I intended, then perform the task satisfactorily?

When we look at it this way, 20 percent sounds pretty good, doesn't it?

If we are coaching a team member on the same thing repeatedly, before we get frustrated with them, we need to ask ourselves, "Am I inspiring better performance or am I just checking this off my list?" "Is there a way I can change my approach on coaching to get a better outcome?"

As the retention scale below illustrates, inspiring extraordinary results requires just a little extra time and effort. We generally remember:

90% of what we both say and do (simulating the real thing, doing the real thing)

70% of what we say (participating in a discussion, giving a talk)

50% of what we hear and see (watching a movie, looking at an exhibit, watching a demonstration)

30% of what we see (looking at pictures)

20% of what we hear (instructions)

10% of what we read (memos, books)

It only takes a few minutes extra to move up this scale to improve coaching effectiveness to prevent re-coaching. For example, instead of giving a team member a new policy or process to read (10 percent retention), you can ask him/her to read it then get back to you later today to explain their interpretation of it and what changes they need to make as a result. Now we are at 70 percent retention (of what we say). That's a good return for your invested time.

Coaching is a pay-me-now or pay-me-later leadership proposition. Take a shortcut and you will be saying the same thing to the same team member next week – no fun for either of you. Do it correctly, and you inspire higher performance and competence … and competence builds confidence. Team confidence is a vital asset for any leader who wants to elevate performance.

Inspiring leaders prevent re-coaching by investing the time to coach right the first time.

Where on the retention scale does most of my coaching interaction fall?

_____

_____

_____

How can I approach my next coaching opportunity to maximize retention and minimize re-coaching?

_____

_____

_____

"I won't accept anything less than the best a player's capable of doing, and he has the right to expect the best that I can do for him and the team."

– LOU HOLTZ

Commitment

• • • • •

Whether it's helping a friend through a tough time, coaching a Little League team, working on a critical project or rebuilding a relationship, **giving our best always gets the best results.**

The moment we totally commit ourselves and begin giving 100 percent, a certain momentum develops. People naturally gravitate to those who are fully committed and start working in the same direction. Total commitment results in a certain, magical boldness – a boldness that has magnetism and power.

Andrew Carnegie said, "The average person puts only 25 percent of his energy and ability into his work. The world takes off its hat to those who put in more than 50 percent of their capacity and stands on its head for those few and far between souls who devote 100 percent." **We compete against our own potential every day.**

I personally experienced the power of 100 percent commitment (and lack thereof!) when I wrestled with publishing my first book for two years. I was consulting and writing leadership articles, and so I thought it might also be time to write a book. I went through all the motions, from working with agents to sending proposals to writers' conferences, but I never seemed to turn the corner from aspiring writer to a published author. There always seemed to be an obstacle, although I now realize it was a result of my less-than-full commitment to my goal.

One obstacle after another … two years and counting. Then one day, I was at a client's office when I saw a big box filled with practical handbooks sitting on a desk. I quickly flipped through one of them and jotted down the publisher's name as I said to myself, "I can do this!" That was my defining moment of commitment. That commitment turned into action, and with the incredibly gracious support of the publisher, I had my first book in print six months later. I was able to envision possibilities that I could only see through fully committed eyes.

Our commitment to our teams can have the same transforming effect. Committed leadership inspires committed teams. During one of the most challenging times in history for the airline industry, for example, Southwest Airlines' team voluntarily forfeited $5 million in vacation time and $1 million in pay to help the company stay financially viable. Team members also took over the lawn and facility maintenance at corporate headquarters. These teams were simply reflecting a deep commitment – personal and professional – they felt from their leadership. When we lead with 100 percent commitment, this is the kind of commitment we can inspire in return.

Even with 100 percent commitment, however, leadership is not always a smooth flight. If we want to pilot our teams to higher levels, we have to understand we can't just kick back in a comfy first-class seat. Now we have responsibility for not only ourselves but also for the safety and success of our teams. They are depending on us to set a good course, keep them posted on our progress and make smart decisions.

Jumping into the pilot's seat brings many more responsibilities than privileges. But those who are defined by their 100 percent commitment reap the rewards of flying high above the rest.

I am continually amazed at the difference between 99 percent and 100 percent commitment. Consider a hot pot of water that is at 211 degrees Fahrenheit. Just one degree hotter and that water hits the boiling point of 212 degrees. Boiling water creates steam and steam can power a huge locomotive. So, that one degree makes the difference between a simple pot of hot water and a real driving force. That one degree of commitment can make an equivalent difference for you and your team.

To which project or task do I need to boost my commitment to 100 percent before I can expect better results?

_____

_____

_____

To which relationship do I need to give my full commitment to inspire extraordinary results?

_____

_____

_____

"Unless commitment is made,
   there are only promises and hopes;
         but no plans."

— PETER DRUCKER

Communication

● ● ● ● ●

What's the one thing leaders do more than anything else
that's the same thing that can always be improved?
Answer: Communication.

Melissa Reiff, President of The Container Store, a
perennially top-ranked company on the *Fortune 100
Best Companies to Work For* summed up the importance
of communication when she said, "Leadership is
communication." And the most critical and influential
communication occurs between a leader and his/her
direct team.

To avoid overcomplicating the communication process, here are three simple steps to inspire extraordinary results: Explain, Ask and Involve.

1. **Explain** expected performance levels, the team's vision and roles. **An explanation gap leads to an execution gap.** Fill that gap by giving your team the data they need to get the job done and to anticipate the future so they do not go to less reliable sources to fill in the missing information.

2. **Ask** employees what they think so they can start participating in the discussion. The key here is to LISTEN. **Don't ask if you're not going to listen.** Asking without listening only builds cynicism, and ultimately a disengaged team. If you don't listen, you don't learn. That goes for any area of life, but particularly with your team.

3. **Involve** employees in creating solutions to problems and finding new opportunities to improve team performance. **People support what they help create.**

In today's hyper-speed, data-overloaded world, we cannot expect to communicate important messages one time and expect it to be understood, internalized and acted upon.

Most teams are too stretched to enable them to change their behavior after hearing something just one time. That's why inspiring leaders use the "Rule of 6" – they communicate important messages at least six times to affect sustained behavior change. They use different methods, but they keep communicating with their teams around the same topic until it becomes a new team habit. So, the three-step process of Explain, Ask, Involve must be repeated again ... and again.

 Take a free *Communication Check-up* and receive a real-time feedback report. theLgroup.com/LeadershipMatters

Which of the three communication steps do I do well?

_____

_____

_____

Which one can I improve upon?

_____

_____

_____

What baby step can I take today to communicate more effectively and inspire extraordinary results?

_____

_____

_____

"*Communicate,*
　　　Communicate,
　　　　　Communicate –
　　until you are sick of hearing yourself.
　　Then *communicate* some more."

– JACK WELCH,
former CEO of General Electric

Connections

● ● ● ● ●

How often do you hear people speak with envy about companies with "real heart"? Companies like Starbucks, Ben & Jerry's, Southwest Airlines, Harley-Davidson, Nordstrom, The Container Store, Apple, FedEx, Fossil and Google, to name a few. Outsiders are constantly looking for their "secrets" to success.

The secret lies in the hearts of their teams. That connectedness is what drives extraordinary results. These teams have strong, intangible connections that yield tangible results.

I remember observing a tangible benefit of connections. I was touring the distribution operation of a national retailer that is well known for building highly connected teams. As my host and I approached the receiving dock, I saw a young worker, maybe 20 years old, waving frantically to the truck that was just pulling away from the dock. He got the driver's attention and waved him back to the dock. Then he quickly grabbed a broom and swept out the floor of the rig, then just as frantically waved the driver off as he yelled, "OK, you're good to go. Thanks!"

Since I was there observing their work processes, this intrigued me, so I approached the young receiving clerk and introduced myself. I asked Lance to describe what had just happened. As he puffed, he said, "Well, that truck is headed to our main store where one of my teammates, Ross, is doing a rotation. Ross has a new baby at home and has had a tough few months, plus he just started this new rotation and he's learning the procedures on the store side. Anyway, I just wanted to make it a little easier for him when the truck arrived. This way, you know, he won't have to sweep out the truck on his end."

Now, that's the power of a connected team! This seemingly extraordinary act of service by Lance was actually the norm at this company because its leaders have taken the time to build connected teams. They do it because they, like other inspiring leaders, believe it's the right thing to do. As a byproduct, these connections yield discretionary effort – teams willingly give their extra time and effort to achieve team goals.

Want results tomorrow? Connect with your team today.

Most of us are so technologically connected that we couldn't disconnect if we tried lest we stare down the dark tunnel of technology withdrawals. But I am talking about connecting vs. being connected.

We live in a hi-tech world but leadership is still a high-touch job. At the risk of being accused of being old school (no risk to me as I am nearly ancient to my kids), let me suggest a simple way to create real connections with our teams, and anyone else for that matter. These are the kinds of connections of which winning relationships are made. I call it QC^2 (sounds pretty hip to me). It's a simple tool to initiate connections – human being to human being.

Question – Asking questions is the least used and most powerful leadership tool you have. Asking questions is selfless and self-serving at the same time. It demonstrates interest in your team while providing you with insights into someone else's world – their motivations, passions, challenges, assumptions and aspirations. Once you ask, make sure you listen. Don't ask if you won't listen – that's the fast track to employee cynicism. **Leaders who really connect listen at least 50 percent of the time** ... and most of the remaining time they are asking questions. Keep it simple by asking things like:

○ How can I help you?

○ What type of project gets you really excited?

○ When do you feel like you are in the zone?

○ What's one thing you would change to improve your work process?

○ What's your vision for this project?

○ What would you like to do less of?

Common Ground – We spend at least eight hours a day with our teams, so we have plenty of topics in common with them. Find common ground as a platform for building a relationship or even a bridge to mend a relationship. When we really observe, watch, ask, listen, it's easy to find things in common. This is more about our mindset than it is about reality. Consider two people who are at odds and walk away from negotiations as a lost cause. Then a mediator walks in and quickly finds a win-win solution.

The contentious parties are focusing on differences while the mediator is focused on commonalities.

Compliment – We do more for those who appreciate us. As long as our compliments are sincere and meaningful, we can pile them on. A sincere compliment is the quickest way to turn an enemy into an ally, a frown into a smile and resistance into acceptance. Look for things your team members are doing right. In addition, look inside of them to find a trait you admire. Are they punctual? Creative? Well-dressed? Optimistic? Intuitive? Willing to do the right thing? Putting the team before themselves? Serving others in the community? There are abundant opportunities to sincerely compliment your team members for who they are and for the impact they have.

Old school or new school, sometimes the basics work best. Forget about connecting through T1 lines, next generation networks and Wi-Fi. Use QC^2 to really connect!

Who on my team do I need to really connect with to build a deeper, more productive relationship?

_____

_____

_____

Which of the QC^2 components am I most comfortable using to connect with others?

_____

_____

_____

Which QC^2 component can I try to use more frequently?

_____

_____

_____

"People will forget what you said,

people will even forget what you did,

people will never forget

how you made them feel."

– MAYA ANGELOU

day 8

Courage

Taking a stand, for anything, requires courage. **Courage is knowing what's right and then acting on it.**

During the Nazi occupation of his country in WWII, King Christian X of Denmark noticed a Nazi flag flying over a Danish public building. He immediately called the German commandant, demanding that the flag be taken down at once. The commandant refused. "Then a soldier will go and take it down," said the king.

"He will be shot," threatened the commandant. "I think not," replied the king, "for I shall be the soldier." Within minutes the flag was taken down. The king was courageous, took his stand and he prevailed.

Inspiring leaders don't settle for what conditions are forced upon them. They don't just buy into what everybody else is saying, and they don't follow the beaten path. Inspiring leaders are constantly creating their own conditions for success by blazing new trails.

Courage is doing something you are afraid to do. The word "courage" is derived from the Medieval Old French term "corage," meaning "heart and spirit."

Howard Schultz, CEO of Starbucks, applied this definition and took his stand when Starbucks wanted to move into a particular international market. Schultz was discouraged by every analysis he read, and spent over a half a million dollars on consultants, who all told him not to go. Further, all of his direct reports were against the move.

On the advice of one of his mentors, Warren Bennis, he met again with his team, listening to their concerns, answering their questions and asking for their support. In the end, he had mobilized the support of his management team, and as Bennis had encouraged, he went with his heart, with what he thought was right and entered the market in question. Schultz stood his ground and, ultimately, was able to score another successful expansion of Starbucks into the international marketplace.

Rarely are leadership decisions black or white, so inspiring leaders take in available data, then muster the courage to make the best decision in that moment for the right reasons.

When did I demonstrate leadership courage in the past?

_____

_____

_____

What about that situation enabled me to act with courage?

_____

_____

_____

How can I apply my past experience to help me courageously address a current challenge?

_____

_____

_____

"In a moment of decision,
        the best thing you can do
                is the right thing.
The worst thing you can do is nothing."
— THEODORE ROOSEVELT

Focus

Consider two sources of energy: the sun and a laser. The sun is a powerful source of energy. It showers the earth with billions of kilowatts of energy every hour. Yet with minimal protection – say a hat and some sunscreen – you can bask in the sunlight for hours with few negative effects. On the other hand, a laser uses a weak source of energy and *focuses* it in a cohesive stream of light, producing intense heat and power. With a laser, you can drill a hole in a diamond or treat certain cancers. That's the power of focus!

It works the same for your team. **Laser-like goals require less energy to yield greater results.** Clarity helps your team succeed because they can better prioritize their time and energy to focus on things that are most important.

If focus is so powerful and productive, why do so many leaders struggle with diffused employee efforts? Today's change-intensive, information-loaded business world creates so many distractions that it's hard for teams (and leaders) to stay focused on their most important goals. These distractions steal time and energy and blur the line of sight between our daily tasks and what's most important to our team. As a result, activity can get mistaken for productivity.

I recently read this saying on a poster: "When winds of change blow hard enough, even the most trivial of objects can become deadly projectiles." Inspiring leaders consistently define and refine their team's focus to help them see clearly through the winds of change ... and achieve extraordinary results.

Diffusion of effort is the enemy of focus ... and success. **The most important decision for a leader is to decide what is most important.** Less important tasks should never steal resources from the most important task. Therefore, our focus cannot be 10 things or five things or even two things. Every team has *one thing* that is most important.

That one thing, if achieved, enables everything else to fall into place.

Your team's focus might be: producing defect-free products; providing the fastest service available; developing leading-edge products; creating relationships that customers cannot walk away from; or meeting the technology needs of other departments. These are just examples – your focus has to be *your* focus. And it should guide all your decisions and actions.

A laser-sharp focus does not happen overnight. It takes time and effort to define, refine, reinforce and communicate your focus, but it needs to start now.

Is my team's focus clear to all of my team members?

_____

_____

_____

What do I need to change to have a more laser-like focus
for my team?

_____

_____

_____

What tasks or initiatives must I say "No" to so my team can
stay focused on what's most important?

_____

_____

_____

"Concentrate all your thoughts
upon the work at hand.
The sun's rays do not burn
until brought to a focus."
– ALEXANDER GRAHAM BELL

Goals

• • • • •

Like many of us, I learned about goal setting early in my career. However, it was only a few years ago that I experienced firsthand the true power of goals. It came at the hands of someone quite small. My middle daughter was seven at the time. She loved to play catch, and I did also. The object we threw did not matter: a tennis ball, football or one of those squishy balls (her personal favorite). It was the challenge of consecutive catches that mattered very much to her.

There was always the same goal, and only one goal, when we played catch: to break the existing records for consecutive catches.

I remember one day when my focused little daughter said, "Dad, let's try for 100 in a row."

Since our best at that point was 50, I politely chuckled and said, "Sure, honey." And guess what, after a few attempts, we did it!

So, the next day she said, "Dad let's go for 300 in a row."

Well, my daughter was learning about thinking big, but I still had a lot to learn. I thought to myself, "Gee, we just hit 100. Why not try 125 or maybe 150 in a row? But 300?" Of course, out loud I responded with another uneasy chuckle and a "Sure, honey."

You guessed it. It was only a few days later that we hit 300 catches in a row. I was really impressed and quite content. My daughter was neither impressed nor content, and she was also a lot smarter than me. She said, "Dad, let's go for 500 now!"

And I thought to myself, "You have GOT to be kidding!"

Sure enough, that very same day, we caught 500 throws in a row. You'd think I would be a believer by now, but when her sparkling eyes looked at me and said, "Dad, let's go for 1,000 in a row!" I am embarrassed to admit that my internal response was the same.

Less than 24 hours later we hit our record – 1,017 catches in a row!

Our record was over 10 times bigger that I had originally thought we could achieve. Thanks to my 7-year-old daughter, I have finally learned to set BIG goals.

So, here's what I learned: **We are only as big and successful as our goals.**

What is an important goal my team is working toward right now?

_____

_____

_____

What is stopping me from increasing it?

_____

_____

_____

"*If you can dream it, you can do it.*"

— WALT DISNEY

Growth

• • • • •

Letting go of old habits isn't easy. As my friend Byrd Baggett says, **"You have to let go to grow."**

Comfort certainly has its advantages – our comfy chair in the living room, a comfortable routine at work, a comfortable relationship. With all the advantages of comfort, here are some things you should know about the comfort zone.

The comfort zone is where most of life is played. It is certainly where most of sports is played. Consider a football field: 90 percent of the game is played between the 20-yard lines. That's why they call anything outside that area the "red zone" – it's where the difference in the game is made.

It's where we really grow personally and our team's score grows! Staying in the comfort zone too long can also get boring, and it stunts our growth.

But, it feels safe in the comfort zone, doesn't it? We know the boundaries, the landscape, and the other comfortable players in the comfort zone. There is little or no risk; a misstep here or there is not very costly. But like the football team that's trapped between the 20-yard lines, we cannot win in the comfort zone. Because the risk is small, so is the reward. **Most learning and growth occur when we are uncomfortable.** Think of the defining moments of growth in your life. Were you hanging out in your comfort zone? No, you were hanging over the edge.

Here are four comforting questions to encourage your growth.

Who else has done it? You may think you're in unexplored territory, but it's unlikely that you're trying something that no one else has ever tried. Look around to find others who have explored the same edge that you might be anxious about. Whether your comfort zone ends at the edge of learning a new skill, speaking in public, making a financial investment, expressing your feelings, or quitting a bad habit, someone else has been at that very same edge. That person can help support you, prepare you, and encourage you to win.

Can I dip my toe in first? You do not have to dive in head first into every new endeavor. Try it out first. Start small. When you reflect on the first time you tried anything new (leading, speaking, rock climbing, painting, playing a musical instrument), you probably remember how uncomfortable you felt. But you stepped out and did it, and you soon discovered that it wasn't as hard as you had expected, right? After a while, what was once in the red zone becomes your comfort zone as you build your competence …

How bad can it be? Often, the fear in your mind paints a picture of things outside your comfort zone as being darker than they really are. Remember, the victory is in the exploration itself more than the success of your attempt.

How great can it be? Your goals are usually bigger than your comfort zone. You must be so passionate about your goals that, instead of feeling that you have to leave your comfort zone, you are magnetically drawn into the red zone to claim victory.

Leaders who "grasp the past" are quickly left right there … in the past. Inspiring leaders continually grow themselves, and their teams are catapulted into a brighter future.

What's one area of personal growth I can work on today?

_____

_____

_____

What is one area of leadership growth I can work on today?

_____

_____

_____

 Watch these inspiring, 2-minute videos
to help you and your team grow.
theLgroup.com/LeadershipMatters

"The greatest thing is, at any moment,
to be willing to give up
who we are in order to
become all
that we can become."

– MAX DE PREE

Humility

· ● ● ● ·

In today's world of boastful athletes, it seems that humility is a lost trait. But the 2006 Winter Olympics in paticular offer a shining example for athletes and business leaders, alike.

For 14 days every four years, the Winter Olympics draws thousands of journalists to capture the triumphs of hundreds of athletes on ski runs, bobsled tracks, ice rinks and snowboard courses.

Each medal awards ceremony connects with the public's admiration and national pride as athletes representing their home countries take the top step of the awards podium and that country's flag is raised to the strains of the appropriate national anthem.

Without a doubt, everyone loves a winner, but there are also a few winning athletes who use their accomplishments to focus the eyes of the world – if only for a moment – on the needs of the less fortunate … and, in doing so, display humility, perhaps, in its purist form.

When Joey Cheek, representing the USA in speed skating, won the 500-meter competition in 2006, he graciously accepted the gold medal and then made these remarks to the media:

> "I have always felt if I ever do something big like this, I want to be able to give something back. I love what I do; it's great fun, but honestly, it's a pretty ridiculous thing. I skate around in tights. If you keep it in perspective, I've trained my whole life for this, but it's not that big a deal.

> "But because I skated well, I have a few seconds of microphone time. And I know how news cycles work. Tomorrow there will be another gold medalist. So I can either gush about how wonderful I feel or use it for something.

> "So I am donating the entire (winning) sum the USOC gives me ($25,000) to an organization, 'Right

to Play,' that helps refugees in Chad, where there are over 60,000 persons displaced from their homes. I am going to be asking all of the Olympic sponsors if they will match my donation."

Cheek went on to win a second medal, a silver in the 1,000 meters, and elected to give the $15,000 bonus he earned from the Olympic committee to the same cause.

In a recap of the 2006 Olympic activities, one commentator mentioned Cheek's $40,000 donation. "It may be that Joey Cheek's humility on the awards podium and the contribution of his medal bonuses to a worthwhile cause may set the stage for more Olympic athletes to do the same in the future."

After the 2006 Olympics concluded, companies around the world had donated a total of $300,000 to match Cheek's contributions.

Humility is not thinking less of ourselves but thinking of ourselves less, like Joey Cheek did. Inspiring leadership, in any venue, is about other people … not us. If we are fortunate enough to build a great team, we will all excel. Staying humble enables us to use our leadership platform to take a stand and conquer much more as a team than we could alone. Humility is not only a desirable trait in leaders, but it is also the fuel for inspiring leaders.

Humility is expressed in our actions, not our words. We cannot afford to be like the guy who was a member of a nationwide, professional association of leaders in the workforce. He was voted the most humble leader in the entire association for leaders. The association presented him with a medal that said, "The most humble leader in America." Then they took it away from him at their next meeting because he wore it!

It's normal to feel proud of a personal accomplishment, but humble leaders take more pride in their team's accomplishment. Pride can turn into a slippery slope of egotism and arrogance. Inspiring leadership requires courage to conquer the outside forces and humility to conquer our inside forces.

When my team succeeds, do I automatically give them full credit when I tell others about the success?

_____

_____

_____

What is one small step I can take today to refocus my efforts on others rather than myself?

_____

_____

_____

"To become truly great,
one has to stand with people,
not above them."

– MARLEEN CHARLES DE MONTESQUIEU

Humor

• • • • •

Natural disasters, disease, war, interpersonal conflict, demanding customers, rising costs. No laughing matters for sure … well, maybe. I contend that facing adversity 100 percent seriously won't help you reverse the situation any faster, so you might as well laugh a little along the way. An upturned mouth is a must in down times. Plus, laughter is free!

In that spirit, here are a few of my favorite one-liners from comedian Steven Wright:

○ "If at first you don't succeed, then skydiving definitely isn't for you."

○ "If you think nobody cares about you, try missing a couple of payments."

○ "My mechanic told me, 'I couldn't repair your brakes, so I made your horn louder.'"

○ "It's not an optical illusion. It just looks like one."

Now, doesn't that feel better?

Most events in our lives do not carry an overwhelming sense of sadness or delight. Most fall into the gray zone of ordinary life, and they present us with a choice: to laugh or not to laugh. Hmm, laughter as a choice?

Laughter is certainly the shortest distance between two people. It unites us, especially when we laugh together. Laughter can heal our relationships ... and even heal us. **Humor is an emotional medicine that can lower stress and diffuse anger.** Our mood is elevated by striving to find humor in difficult and frustrating situations. Laughing at ourselves and the situation helps reveal that small things are not the earth-shaking events they sometimes seem to be. Looking at a problem from a different perspective can make it seem less formidable and provides opportunities for greater objectivity and insight.

Below are four simple strategies to help tickle your funny bone more frequently.

1. Appreciate Life's Extremes.

If your situation seems ridiculously frustrating, recognize the potential humor in just how ridiculously frustrating and annoying it is. In your imagination, take the situation to an extreme that becomes even more ridiculous until you find yourself amused. You know, picture a Steve Martin or Adam Sandler movie.

2. Focus on Humor.

Do you know someone who always seems to have drama going on in his/her life? Like they are living in a soap opera? It's really a matter of what they choose to focus on. We can just as easily focus on the humorous things we see and experience each day, and all of a sudden, our life is a comedy!

3. Find a Funny Friend.

Find a friend with whom you can laugh. You can each share your frustrations, and laugh about them in the process. Even when your friend isn't there, you can lighten your mood in a dark situation by thinking about the retelling that will come later.

4. Watch Funny Shows and Movies.

No doubt, there are plenty of not-so-funny shows and movies. However, classic shows like *The Office* and *Seinfeld* take universal situations that we find frustrating and push them a little further, pointing out just how goofy it all is. Realizing that some universally annoying situations are actually funny can help you endure them with a smile.

OK, since I heard your laughter earlier, here is an encore performance from Steven Wright. This time with his classic quizzical questions ….

"OK, so what's the speed of dark?"

"How do you tell when you're out of invisible ink?"

"What happens if you get scared half to death twice?"

We all want to enjoy our work, and humor has a funny way of creating good times.

What is a particularly frustrating or challenging situation my team is currently dealing with?

_____

_____

_____

Which of the four humor strategies can I use to lighten the mood around that situation?

_____

_____

_____

"It is a curious fact
        that people are never
                so trivial as when they
take themselves seriously."

– OSCAR WILDE

Impact

● ● ● ● ●

Contrary to the lyrics from a classic rock song, one is not the loneliest number. But it is the most important number!

Your thoughts, words, and actions are like individual notes that work in concert to create the power of one person, you, to make a difference.

You can harness your full personal impact by taking just one step:

○ Catch one negative thought and turn it into a positive one;

○ Think of one thing for which you are grateful at the beginning of each day;

○ Say one "Fantastic!" when a colleague asks how you are doing;

○ Assume the best in one upcoming challenging interaction;

○ Keep on moving one step at a time when you experience adversity;

○ Help one colleague during a time when you need help.

Many people used to think that one vote in an election couldn't really make a difference. Well, past presidential elections that have been decided by razor-thin margins prove them wrong. **A single act does make a difference … it creates a ripple effect that can be felt many miles and people away.** And as one of my friends pointed out recently, a single positive act creates a powerful internal ripple effect within us – one of good feelings and service to others.

Susan Komen's life provides a current day example of the power of one. When Susan was diagnosed with breast cancer in 1978, little was known about the disease and it was rarely discussed in public. Before her death at age 36, Susan asked her sister Nancy to do everything she could to bring an end to breast cancer. Although Nancy wasn't sure that she alone could accomplish this goal, she kept her promise. In 1982, Nancy established the Susan G. Komen Breast Cancer Foundation with $200 and a shoebox full of names.

In 1983, the first Susan G. Komen "Race for the Cure" was held. It attracted 800 runners and raised several hundred thousand dollars. As of this print, 1.6 million runners participate in more than 140 locations globally for breast cancer research, education, screening and treatment. As a result, the Foundation has invested more than $1.9 billion since its inception to eradicate breast cancer. All this good for the world started with one request to one person who took one action.

All great things start as one small thing. So, take one small step out … and make a positive impact today!

What one small action can I take today to create a
positive impact for someone who is important to me?

_____

_____

_____

What one small action can I take today to create a
positive impact for my team?

_____

_____

_____

"Knowing is not enough;

we must apply.

Willing is not enough;

we must do."

– JOHANN WOLFGANG VON GOETHE

Influence

● ● ● ● ●

A traditional definition of leadership often includes "getting people to follow your vision." However, in today's mega-matrixed world, leaders often do not have direct authority over those they need to help realize their vision. The truly inspiring leader often leads through influence – a more subtle yet powerful approach to getting things done.

One of the most important aspects of influencing others is spreading and soliciting new ideas. That's right, **influence is a two-way street.** The influential leader is a conduit of ideas – some are his while others are from his team. Some are well-baked concepts and validated theories while others are raw musings and trial balloons. Sometimes it's about listening while other times it's about speaking. Your focus might be on brainstorming today and on refining tomorrow. This is woven into lots of informal interactions vs. formal meetings. Some interactions might be more in-depth, but most of them are simply about connecting with people for no immediate business reason. Most discussions take about 10 minutes and can be stimulated by questions/comments like:

- What do you think about this idea I have?

- How would you deal with X challenge or initiative?

- What's the first thing you would do if you had my job?

- What's on your dream list of things to work on?

- I would like you to participate in X meeting (one they would not normally participate in) and share your thoughts.

- I would like you to share my idea with your teammates, see what they think, then give me completely unfiltered feedback.

Rather than schedule these interactions (it can feel too formal and potentially stifling), budget five to 10 minutes before a meeting each day to zigzag your way to the meeting (or even to the restroom or lunch). Pop in on team members and strike up a conversation using some of the suggestions or your own version of them.

You can even add in a lunch once in a while with someone you would not typically have lunch with, a team member a couple of levels below you or in another department. Slow and steady as you watch your influence grow. Today, the world of work is no longer a simple cause (manager commands) and effect (employee reacts), so inspiring leaders use influence to inspire extraordinary results.

Who is one person I need to establish more influence with?

_____

_____

_____

What would I like to ask them or discuss with him?

_____

_____

_____

When will I have this discussion?

_____

_____

_____

"The secret of my influence has always been that it remained secret."

– SALVADOR DALI

Integrity

Without a doubt, your personal integrity is your most prized possession. Each day, that integrity is constantly tested, and you have an opportunity to prove it or lose it with every decision you make.

Integrity is also the most fundamental leadership characteristic. Consider this: **Without integrity, people will not follow you, and if you have no followers, you are not leading.**

Doing the right thing is not always the easiest thing – but it is always the right thing to do. Choosing to do the right thing – even when it's painful – ensures you will maintain this most precious possession throughout your leadership journey.

The word "integrity" stems from the Latin adjective *integer*, meaning "whole, complete." In this context, integrity is the inner sense of "wholeness" deriving from qualities such as honesty and consistency of character. In short, since we are always leading and our teams are always watching us, we must do what we say and say what we do.

This poem by Frank Outlaw appears on a poster in my son's room, so I see it every day. It eloquently illustrates the need for personal integrity:

> Watch your thoughts;
>
> > They become your words.
>
> Watch your words;
>
> > They become your actions.
>
> Watch your actions;
>
> > They become your habits.
>
> Watch your habits;
>
> > They become your character.
>
> Watch your character;
>
> > It becomes your destiny.

Your integrity is your greatest asset, personally and professionally. Losing it is the quickest way to halt your success. There is no gray area when it comes to integrity. Inspiring leaders control every thought, every word and every action to serve as a magnificent reflection of integrity for their teams.

Who can I fully trust to tell me when my integrity
is slipping?

_____

_____

_____

When is the soonest I can check in with him/her?

_____

_____

_____

"Never separate
    the life you live
        from the words you speak."
                                    – PAUL WELLSTONE

Intuition

● ● ● ● ●

Tom Peters called intuition our greatest gift. It's the feeling we get when what we are seeing doesn't match up with the facts we think we know; it's the sudden move we make without thinking that saves us from disaster; it's the voice that tells us the truth rather than what we would like to hear.

Intuition can help us make quick and sound decisions based on a minimum of information. For instance, take a look at this paragraph …

> Cna yuo raed tihs? I cdn'uolt blveiee taht I cluod aulaclty uesdnatnrd waht I was rdanieg. The phaonemnel pweor of the hmuan mnid, aoccdrnig

to a rsereeachr at Cmabrigde Uinervtisy, it dseno't mtaetr in waht oerdr the ltteres in a wrod are, the olny iproamtnt tihng is taht the frsit and lsat ltteers be in the rghit pclae. The rset can be a taotl mses and you can sitll raed it whotuit a pboerlm. Tihs is bcuseae the huamn mnid deos not raed ervey lteter by istlef, but the wrod as a wlohe. Azanmig, huh? Yaeh, and I awlyas tghuhot slpeling was ipmorantt!

Isn't it astounding how easily we can decipher words with information that is ambiguous, garbled, or less than complete? We are wired to see underlying patterns, fill in the gaps, straighten out the miscues, and discover the hidden meanings. The same is true of our innate ability to make decisions.

Applying the 80/20 Rule to our thinking can help us make smarter, faster, more intuitive decisions. The 80/20 Rule is pervasive in our world:

○ 80% of traffic jams occur on 20% of roads.

○ 80% of beer is consumed by 20% of drinkers.

○ 80% of classroom participation comes from 20% of students.

○ 80% of profits come from 20% of customers.

In most situations, you can gather 80 percent of the relevant information in the first 20 percent of the time available. Generally, the remaining 20 percent of the data (which would take the remaining 80 percent of your time to obtain) would not substantially improve the quality of your decision. Your intuition is good enough to organize the data and fill in the gaps, just as it did in the nonsense paragraph above.

Specifically, here's how you might apply the 80/20 Rule to your next decision. First, identify the top five pieces of information you need to make the decision. Then, decide which four of these five are highest in priority. Once you've gathered this information, you will have roughly 80 percent of the information you need, and the remaining 20 percent is less important. Now, harness all of your experience and your intuition to fill in the blanks and make a great decision – even faster. So, quit analyzing and follow your intuition.

What is a decision I currently need to make?

_____

_____

_____

What are the most critical pieces of information I need to make it?

_____

_____

_____

"Intuition is the supra-logic
that cuts out all the routine
processes of thought and
leaps straight from
the problem to the answer."

— ROBERT GRAVES

Investment

● ● ● ● ●

Two young men were working their way through Stanford University in the late 1890s when, during the semester, their funds got desperately low. So, they came up with the idea of engaging Ignacy Paderewski, the great pianist, for a recital. After paying the concert expenses, the two students could use the profits to pay their board and tuition.

The great pianist's manager asked for a guarantee of $2,000. The students, undaunted, proceeded to stage the concert. But alas, the concert raised only $1,600.

After the performance, the students sought the great artist, gave him the entire $1,600, a promissory note for

$400, and explained they would earn the remainder of his fee and send the money to him.

"No," replied Paderewski, "that won't do." Then tearing the note to shreds, he returned the money and said to them, "Now, take out of this $1,600 all of your expenses and keep for each of you 10 percent of the balance for your work."

The years rolled by – years of fortune and destiny. Paderewski had become Premier of Poland. The devastating war came, and Paderewski's only focus was to feed the starving thousands in his beloved Poland. Yet just as the need was most severe, thousands of tons of food began to come into Poland for distribution by the Polish Premier.

After all the starving people were fed and hard times had past, Paderewski journeyed to Paris to thank Herbert Hoover for the relief he had sent. "That's all right, Mr. Paderewski," was soon-to-be U.S. President Hoover's reply. "You don't remember it, but you helped me once when I was a student at college and I was in a hole. You invested in me … now it's my turn."

Investing in other people, and ourselves, provides a far greater return than the best mutual fund. **Inspiring**

leadership is about pouring ourselves into others and helping them draw out their natural gifts … so they, in turn, can invest in others.

With whom can I invest more time and energy in order to help them reach their full potential?

_____

_____

_____

In what area do I need to invest in to help me reach my own potential?

_____

_____

_____

"An investment in
            knowledge
     always pays
          the best interest."

– BENJAMIN FRANKLIN

Knowledge

● ● ● ● ●

I heard this story about a member of America's "greatest generation" that illustrates the matter of knowledge.

A friend's grandfather came to America from Eastern Europe. After being processed at Ellis Island, he went into a cafeteria in Lower Manhattan. He sat down at an empty table and waited for someone to take his order. Of course nobody did. Finally, a woman with a tray full of food sat down opposite him and informed him how a cafeteria worked.

"Start out at that end," she said. "Just go along the line and pick out what you want. At the other end, they'll tell you how much you have to pay."

"I soon learned that's how everything works in America," the grandfather told my friend. "Life's a cafeteria. You can get anything you want as long as you are willing to pay the price of learning. You can even get success, but you'll never get it if you wait for someone to bring it to you. You have to get up and get it yourself."

Inspiring leadership is not just about investing in others. **Inspiring leadership is also about investing in ourselves.** Today more than ever, there is a cafeteria of learning available to us … and it's filled with the food of knowledge. Your life is a virtual cafeteria of learning where you can build your leadership competence. You can find best practices everywhere. Watch the people around you. You can find nuggets of insight from a father-in-law, a clergyman, a speaker at a professional association meeting, a fellow leader, a mentor, a child, a Boy Scout's troop leader or a particularly helpful salesperson at a local department store. Observe, read, ask, listen and learn.

There are also lessons to be learned in everything your team does. Look for opportunities in post-project reviews, customer meetings, conflicts with other departments, changes in priorities, miscommunications and mistakes. Seize all these experiences to feed yourself and your team. This hones our competence … and **competence builds**

confidence. Confidence is critical – inspiring leaders need it and their teams want to see it.

Your mind is a muscle. Keep learning and it strengthens. Stop learning and it atrophies. Inspiring leaders are hungry to consume knowledge and are just as eager to share it.

Take a moment to invest in yourself and exercise your brain!

What is one source of knowledge I can do a better job of tapping into – a colleague, listening to CDs, a mentor?

_____

_____

_____

Where can I look for good examples of inspiring leadership outside of my work setting?

_____

_____

_____

 Access 250+ free resources to boost your leadership knowledge.
theLgroup.com/LeadershipMatters

"Leadership and
learning are
indispensable to
each other."
– JOHN F. KENNEDY

Legacy

● ● ● ● ●

Inheritance is what we leave *to* others. Legacy is what we leave *in* them.

Here is one of my favorite, true stories of really leaving a legacy.

In the early 1900s, Al Capone virtually owned Chicago. Capone wasn't famous for anything heroic. He was notorious for entangling the Windy City in everything from bootlegged booze and prostitution to murder.

Capone had a lawyer nicknamed "Easy Eddie." He was Capone's lawyer for a good reason. Eddie was very good at what he did. In fact, Eddie's skill at legal maneuvering kept Big Al out of jail for a long time. To show his appreciation, Capone paid him very well.

Not only was the money big, but Eddie also got special dividends. For instance, he and his family occupied a fenced-in mansion with live-in help and all of the conveniences of the day. The estate was so large it filled an entire Chicago city block.

Eddie lived the high life of the Chicago mob and gave little consideration to the serious wrongdoings that went on around him, but he did have one soft spot. He had a son he loved dearly, and Eddie saw to it that his young son had the best of everything – clothes, cars and a good education. Nothing was withheld and price was no object.

Despite his involvement with organized crime, Eddie even tried to teach his son right from wrong. Eddie wanted him to be a better man than he was. Yet with all his wealth and influence, there were two things he couldn't give his son – he couldn't pass on a good name and he couldn't set a good example.

One day, Easy Eddie reached a difficult decision. Wanting to rectify wrongs he had done, he decided he would go to the authorities and tell the truth about Al "Scarface"

Capone, clean up his tarnished name and offer his son some semblance of integrity. To do this, he would have to testify against the Mob, and he knew that the cost would be great. So he testified. Within the year, Easy Eddie's life ended in a blaze of gunfire on a lonely Chicago Street, but in his eyes, he had given his son the greatest gift he had to offer, at the greatest price he would ever pay.

Now, let's fast forward to World War II, a war that produced many heroes. One such man was Lt. Cmdr. Butch O'Hare. He was a fighter pilot assigned to the aircraft carrier Lexington in the South Pacific.

One day, his entire squadron was sent on a mission. After he was airborne, he looked at his fuel gauge and realized that someone had forgotten to top off his fuel tank. He would not have enough fuel to complete his mission and get back to his ship. His flight leader told him to return to the carrier. Reluctantly, he dropped out of formation and headed back to the fleet. As he was returning to the mother ship, he saw something that turned his blood cold. A squadron of Japanese aircraft was speeding their way toward the American fleet.

The American fighters were gone on a sortie, and the fleet was all but defenseless. He couldn't reach his squadron and bring them back in time to save the fleet, nor could he warn the fleet of the approaching danger. There was only one thing to do. He must somehow divert them from the fleet. Laying aside all thoughts of personal safety, he dove into the formation of Japanese planes. Wing-mounted 50 calibers blazed as he charged in, attacking one surprised enemy plane and then another. Butch wove in and out of the now broken formation and fired at as many planes as possible until all his ammunition was finally spent. Undaunted, he continued the assault.

He dove at the planes, trying to clip a wing or tail in hopes of damaging as many enemy planes as possible and rendering them unfit to fly. Finally, the exasperated Japanese squadron took off in another direction.

Deeply relieved, Butch O'Hare and his tattered fighter limped back to the carrier. Upon arrival he reported in and related the event surrounding his return. The film from the gun-camera mounted on his plane told the tale. It showed the extent of Butch's daring attempt to protect his fleet. He had, in fact, destroyed five enemy aircraft. This took place on Feb. 20, 1942, and for that action Butch became the Navy's first Ace of WWII and the first Naval aviator to win the Congressional Medal of Honor. A year later, Butch was killed in aerial combat at the age of 29.

His hometown would not allow the memory of this WWII hero fade, and today, O'Hare Airport in Chicago is named in tribute to the courage of this great man. So the next time you find yourself at O'Hare International, think about visiting Butch's memorial displaying his statue and his Medal of Honor.

So what do these two stories have to do with each other?

Butch O'Hare was Easy Eddie's son.

The life we live today affects the generations to come. We were meant to give away our lives, so focus on living your legacy instead of worrying about leaving your legacy. If you do, you will define yourself and others by an inspired life.

One of the most joyful moments for any leader is to pass the baton to someone we have invested in, and then see our values reflected in the new leader … just like Butch O'Hare.

What legacy do I want to leave my team?

_____

_____

_____

What am I doing today to positively affect someone's life,
not just their work?

_____

_____

_____

● ● ● ● ●

"You give but little
    when you give of your possessions.
    It is when you give of yourself
    that you truly give."

– KAHLIL GIBRAN

Passion

● ● ● ● ●

Happiness comes from following your passion. Excellence comes from work you are passionate about. **Passion enables your team to perform ordinary tasks in extraordinary ways.**

Knowing *what* to do drives performance, but knowing *why* you do it ignites passion. Passion enables your team to find creative ways to achieve a goal … any goal.

Consider most types of sports equipment – a golf club, a tennis racquet, a baseball bat – have a sweet spot that, if the ball hits it, will give the player the optimal result. Hitting this sweet spot yields a long drive down the fairway, a swift cross-court return or homerun swing. Every sport has a sweet spot of some type. If you have experienced it, you know when you hit the sweet spot; you barely feel it. The ball goes where you want it to go … even farther and faster. It doesn't get any better than that! Inspiring leaders help their team members play in their professional sweet spots, leveraging their natural talents.

To help your team find their sweet spots, ensure a good fit between a team member's natural abilities and the requirements of the job – the "highest and best use" of their talents toward your team goals. Wouldn't you love having each team member working in their sweet spot? Gaining insights into your *own* leadership sweet spot helps you better determine how to design roles and utilize team members. For example, if your sweet spot is conceptually designing complex deals, ensure you have a strong analyst on your team for balance. If your sweet spot is analyzing lots of details and numbers, you want some conceptual, big-picture thinkers on your team.

Look at where the answers to these two questions overlap to reveal a sweet spot:

1. What types of work am I absolutely passionate about?

2. Which tasks are very easy and natural for me to perform?

Recall times when you were told that you made it look easy, that you really excelled and you looked like you were having a blast. What were you doing?

Ignite your passion; inspire extraordinary results.

What is my leadership "sweet spot"?

_____

_____

_____

What skills do I need on my team to balance my skills?

_____

_____

_____

 Take a free *Passionate Performance*
Profile and receive a real-time
feedback report.
theLgroup.com/LeadershipMatters

"Chase your passion
         not your pension."

– DENIS WAITLEY

Perseverance

When I was a senior in high school, I participated in a mock congress with fellow seniors from throughout the state of Florida in a program called Boys' State. It was held in Tallahassee, the state capital and hosted at Florida State University, which eventually become my alma mater. More importantly, it provided a first-hand lesson in perseverance for me. Let me explain.

During the course of the week at the state capital in Tallahassee, we learned about legislative issues, primarily by acting them out and holding mock elections for a variety of political offices. So I figured, "Hey, I'm only here once. Why not just go for it?" So I ran for a lower-level position the second day, but lost to another student. No problem, I can take rejection. So I tried for a slightly higher office the next day, but I lost again. Now the stakes got higher – more prestigious offices on the line and a bruised ego that needed repair. I tried again but no victory. The next day again … nope! I have to win at some point, right? So one more time I submitted my petition, made the rounds, and cast my vote. Votes finally came and I kept my perfect record: 0 wins, 5 losses.

Well, now we were down to the last day of the program and only the highest offices were left to be filled – the Governor's cabinet. Here's where the real campaigning kicks in. Pressing flesh, addressing the issues, oh yea, and making a speech in front of 1,000 of my fellow students (most of whom had won some type of office by now). With five defeats under my belt, there was nothing much left to lose.

With shaking knees and sweating palms, I made my first big speech (thank goodness for lecterns!) as I ran for Commissioner of Education. I decided to make perseverance one of my issues – it certainly seemed relevant, to me at least. All told, at least I left the week with a 1-and-5 record, but my one victory was the one that really counted. As Thomas Edison said, "**Genius?**

Nothing! Sticking to it is the genius! … I've failed my way to success."

Unfortunately, most people fail because they don't stick to it long enough to succeed. Fortunately for me, at that young age, I was naïve enough to keep pushing forward in spite of my failures. Sticking to it long enough to win is a common defining moment for many leaders. These moments are so memorable because they often test our faith in ourselves and our teams.

Since we cannot always see the tangible results of our leadership, we must trust that doing the right things will yield the desired results. We demonstrate this faith in everyday things, but somehow it seems more challenging with our teams.

The life of an inspiring leader works much the same way. Sometimes, it might seem as though our teams are going through their own "dark room" experience before we finally see the positive results of our efforts. Trust that your efforts will yield the excellence you pursue. And against all odds … persevere!

When have I persevered against all odds to achieve a goal?

_____

_____

_____

What did I do to persevere?

_____

_____

_____

What is one project, goal, or relationship that I need to keep persevering on, having faith that my efforts will eventually pay off?

_____

_____

_____

 Take a free *Adherence Assessment* to measure your team's ability to stick to their plans.
theLgroup.com/LeadershipMatters

"To be a champion you have to
                    believe in yourself
         when no one else will."
                          — SUGAR RAY ROBINSON

Perspective

● ● ● ● ●

As a youngster, I always thought Rose Colan, my beloved mother, originated the phrase, "This too shall pass." She used it frequently to help me keep perspective during challenging times.

Since then, I have learned that this saying appears in the works of Persian poets and in Jewish folklore from King Solomon … quite a few years before I heard my mom say it. The context is from a fable of a powerful king who asks wise men to create a ring that will make him happy when he is sad, and vice versa. After deliberation, the sages handed him a simple ring with the words **"This too will pass"** etched on it, which had the desired effect.

When you are on top of the world, enjoy it and know that things change. Remember, this too shall pass. When you are in the pits, all nights are followed by day; at your lowest moments remember also, this too shall pass. External circumstances and material things change.

I tell our clients, "No trend goes on forever" (my clumsy version of this ancient saying). Although leading a high-performing team certainly has an important emotional component, **inspiring leaders keep an even-keeled perspective**. This balanced perspective prevents complacency in good times and despair in bad times. It also keeps us humble and hopeful, appreciating how circumstances can quickly change. Taking these words to heart will keep your team's edge sharp and their performance peaked.

So, no matter what your circumstances, remember, THIS TOO SHALL PASS!

What is one challenge my team is facing today?

_____

_____

_____

How can I help my team maintain hope for a brighter tomorrow?

_____

_____

_____

"The question
is not what
you look at,
but what you see."

– HENRY DAVID THOREAU

Purpose

• • • • •

Recently, a client of mine was reflecting on a former boss who really understood how to create a sense of purpose. She clearly recalled her first day on the job at a local hospital. Her new boss said, "Cheryl, your job is to create a safe, clean environment to help our patients go home with their families as soon as possible." This got her excited about coming to work. It just so happened that Cheryl created a safe, clean environment by washing dishes, but that was secondary to the sense of purpose that she now had.

All of us are in search of a clear and driving purpose for our lives; we want to contribute to something bigger than ourselves. The world of work offers a great opportunity for people to connect with a purpose. Without a purpose, your team is just putting in time. Their minds might be engaged, but their hearts will not be. A team without a purpose is a team without passion. Your team members may achieve short-term results, but they won't have the heart to go the distance.

A purpose is your team's bridge to a brighter tomorrow … and you have to build it! It is *not* a project goal, financial target or strategic plan. Your team won't get emotionally charged about a "10 percent net profit," a "20 percent return on investment" or a "30 percent increase in market share." A compelling purpose is a reason to be excited about getting up and going to work every day.

A purpose can come in all varieties – perhaps it's to help others, to make the world a better place, to innovate or to win. For example, Disney's purpose is "to make dreams come true." Coke works diligently to develop its purpose: to put a Coke within reach of every person on Earth. Pepsi's purpose is to "beat Coke!" Your organization's real purpose may not be apparent at first glance. For instance, a company that distributes building products to homebuilders may not seem to have a compelling cause; but a deeper look reveals that they "help make the American dream a reality." That's a cause worth working for!

Be bold. Step back and look at the big picture. Think about how your team improves conditions for others. Your purpose should answer the questions, "Why do we exist?" And "How do we improve the lives of others?" It should stir the emotions. Keep it short and sweet – use simple language and keep it to less than 10 words or so.

For example, a customer call center may have a purpose "to brighten the day of each caller by solving a problem." A data security department's cause could be "to ensure confidence by securing customers' most private information." For a human resources department, it might be "to create a family that likes to win together."

Engage your team by asking them how their jobs relate to your team's purpose. Some questions you might pose include:

- ○ "How does our purpose make you feel?" (If you hear responses like *proud, important, connected, helpful* or *like a winner*, then you're on the right track.)

- ○ "Does our purpose make you look at your job differently?"

- ○ "Do our roles, procedures, resources, skills and priorities support our ability to achieve our purpose?"

○ "What can you change or do differently to better support our purpose?"

○ "What can I change or do differently to better support our purpose?"

Inspiring leaders don't depend on chance, they lead on purpose.

What is my team's purpose?

_____

_____

_____

Does the team know and clearly understand its purpose?

_____

_____

_____

Is it emotionally compelling?

_____

_____

_____

"The more you lose yourself
   in something bigger than yourself,
      the more energy you will have."

– NORMAN VINCENT PEALE

Reflection

● ● ● ● ●

Today's hyperactive and attention-demanding world makes reflection no easy task. Nonetheless, we still must find a way to carve out "mental space" so we can think clearly, plan, reflect, dream.

My youngest daughter has a special area in her room where she can chill and relax. She calls it her "chillax zone." Although your chillax zone might not have big pink pillows and a fluffy white carpet, we all need to make a time and place that offers us mental space. Your space might be your car as you drive home after work, a reading or meditation corner in your house, your bathtub, your gym, a nearby park where you walk – anywhere you can be alone with your thoughts. The thinking, planning, and reflection you do in this space helps you get off the treadmill and rise above the daily whirlwind to gain valuable perspective.

Here are some of the ways you can create some mental space:

○ Schedule meetings for 45 minutes instead of one hour to build in time to synthesize your thoughts in-between meetings.

○ Create a recurring, weekly meeting with yourself, even if only 15 minutes, to reflect on your thoughts about yourself, your team and your goals.

○ Turn off your car radio occasionally to think on your way to work or debrief on your way home.

○ Take a walk after lunch to get fresh air, reflect on the morning and get energized for the afternoon.

○ Disconnect from all forms of technology for one hour a week to get back in touch with things and people who are right in front of you.

Not only is a mind a terrible thing to waste, it is a terrible thing to clutter. Find the time and space to free your mind to do what it does best – think.

How can I adjust my schedule to take back at least 15 minutes a day of uninterrupted time to reflect?

_____

_____

_____

When can I turn off background "noise" (e.g., radio, TV, computer screen) for a few minutes to gain some valuable reflection time?

_____

_____

_____

"Follow effective action with quiet reflection. From the quiet reflection will come even more effective action."

– PETER DRUCKER

Self-care

● ● ● ● ●

Can you recite the flight attendant's safety speech? I bet you can. You know, the one that goes something like, "… In the event of a loss of cabin pressure, an oxygen mask will drop from above. If you are traveling with a child, place your mask on first …"

I found this version of the speech made by a flight attendant who was trying to break the boredom and gain the attention of the passengers …

"In the event of a loss of cabin pressure these baggy things will drop down over your head. You stick it over your nose and mouth like the flight attendant is doing now. The bag won't inflate, but there's oxygen there, promise. If you are sitting next to a small child, or someone who is acting like a small child, please do us all a favor and put on your mask first. If you are traveling with two or more children, please take a moment now to decide which one is your favorite. Help that one first, and then work your way down."

As a parent, it always seems counterintuitive to put your own mask on first (not to mention picking your favorite child!). Upon further reflection, I think there is a broader lesson in this speech for any leader – whether you lead a team at work, in the community or at home. It's simple: **Take care of yourself first, so you can better serve others.** This sounds simple, but it's counterintuitive for inspiring leaders who tend to put others' needs before their own.

You are less helpful to those you serve without your own "oxygen mask" – whether your oxygen mask is physical health (rest, diet and exercise), emotional balance, intellectual stimulation, spiritual strength or financial fortitude. If you are running low on oxygen or anything else you need to perform at your peak, you cannot be serving your team optimally. Inspiring leaders generally eat right, exercise, get regular check-ups, read a lot, engage in hobbies and have friends outside of work.

It's what fuels their focus, ideas and drive while they are on the job.

So, next time you feel like you need a breather, take a lesson from your friendly flight attendant, and put your oxygen mask on first. Those you serve will appreciate you being at your best!

Who is depending on me to be my best at work?
At home?

_____

_____

_____

Which areas of my life do I need to take better care of
so that I can better serve those who depend on me?

_____

_____

_____

"A man too busy
      to take care of his health
            is like a mechanic too busy
to take care of his tools."

– SPANISH PROVERB

Significance

● ● ● ● ●

You don't have to become an industrial baron and make a billion dollars to live a life of significance. All you have to do is share the resources you now have. However insignificant you may think they are, your resources are of greater value to someone not so fortunate as you.

The straightforward way to live a life of significance is simply to **share your three T's: time, talent, and treasure.** Our lives are meant to be given away – to significant purposes, to loving families, to friends in need, to lasting relationships. Find a way that your gifts can serve others. Your time, energy, and money are precious resources – they are limited, and you are the sole owner. If you spend them in one area, you can't spend them in another. When we say "yes" to one thing, by default we are saying "no" to something else. The key to winning is to say "yes" to the significant things in your life.

Time. It's a paradox of life that only by giving away our time do we make our lives meaningful, for time is the most precious gift of all. The time we spend playing with a child or grandchild, chatting with a bedridden friend, coaching a team member, supporting a colleague, or serving those in need in our community cannot be measured in dollars but is priceless. And life rewards those who donate their time, first in terms of their own satisfaction and the good opinion of others, later in ways they can never foresee. The time may come when you need a hand, and there will be many more hands offering help than you can count.

Talent. There's something especially rewarding about applying your best talents toward the benefit of others. The way to make the greatest contribution with your talent is by recognizing and using your strengths. Applying your talents to something bigger than yourself – a team's goal, an industry meeting, a professional association or a community project – inspires a sense of meaning and significance.

Treasure. You don't have to be rich to donate your treasure to others – an insignificant part of modest holdings can be a fortune to others – but stories of truly generous wealthy people inspire us. Here's one such story.

In 1981, business leader and self-made millionaire Eugene Lang looked out at the faces of the 59 African-American and Puerto Rican sixth-graders who had come to hear him speak. Years earlier, Lang had attended this same school in East Harlem. Now, he wondered how he could get these children to listen to him. What could he say to inspire these students when, statistically, most would probably drop out of school before graduation?

Finally, scrapping his notes, he spoke from his heart. "Stay in school," he told them. "If you do, I'll help pay the college tuition for every one of you."

At that moment, he changed the life of every student in the room. For the first time, they had hope – hope of achieving more than their older brothers and sisters, hope of living a better life than their parents and neighbors.

Six years later, nearly 90 percent of that class graduated from high school, and true to his promise, Lang made it possible for them to attend college. A few years later he founded the "I Have a Dream" Foundation, which has supported similar projects in 57 cities, assisted by more than 200 sponsors helping more than 12,000 disadvantaged students with academic support and guidance through high school and a college education.

There's a Chinese proverb that says, "If you continually give, you will continually have." A perfect formula for building a significant team and a significant life.

How can I gift my time today to make a significant difference in someone's life?

_____

_____

_____

Which of my natural talents would I enjoy using to serve another person or organization outside of my work?

_____

_____

_____

"Getting what you want
　　　is not nearly as important
　　　　　as giving what you have."

– HENRY DAVID THOREAU

Trust

● ● ● ● ●

Bernard Madoff scammed over 5,000 investors out of approximately $65 billion (yes, that's a billion with a "B"). Like any crime that you read or hear about, it's concerning to each of us. My reaction deepened as I spoke with an old friend whose aging parents had invested all their retirement savings with Madoff. I directly felt their real-life implications of broken trust as my friend's parents considered selling their house, changing a lifestyle they had worked years to earn and became anxious about an uncertain final chapter in their lives.

Trust is the basis for all successful leaders and all successful relationships, for that matter. You cannot buy trust, but it is free. Trust is priceless yet can be earned over time. Have you ever tried to request someone's trust? Maybe it was a team member, customer or a colleague. You may have wanted a decision to be made in your favor. To overcome some initial disagreement and expedite the decision-making process, you might resort to "Hey, just trust me!" That statement is worthless. Either the other party already trusted you based on your past actions or they did not trust you and your request won't change that. **Trust is not spoken, it is demonstrated. Trust cannot be requested, it must be earned.**

We need to earn and nurture our team's trust every day – whether a team at home or work. A trusting team …

- ○ Is more open to change;

- ○ Delivers better service;

- ○ Focuses on finding win-win solutions;

- ○ Has lower turnover;

- ○ Shares unfiltered information to help the team deal with the facts and be successful;

- ○ Quickly forgives their leader if s/he makes a mistake.

Trust can be complex, so here are three simple steps to become more trustworthy:

○ Serve your team's best interests (rather than your own).

○ Communicate all the information your team needs to be successful. Don't make assumptions about what you think they can "handle." Leaders who underestimate the intelligence of their teams tend to overestimate their own.

○ Keep each and every commitment you make to your team. This is tough, so watch your words. Even a casual comment from a leader can be interpreted as a commitment.

We can all improve our trust-building behaviors. Inspiring leaders are bold enough to be honest with themselves and make necessary changes. Now more than ever, your team's success may come down to a matter of trust.

What do I need to more fully communicate to my team to build their trust in me?

_____

_____

_____

Which of my habits or assumptions might prevent me from demonstrating trust in my team?

_____

_____

_____

"Few delights can equal
        the presence of one
                whom we trust utterly."

— GEORGE MACDONALD

Values

● ● ● ● ●

The Leaning Tower of Pisa was constructed in three stages over 177 years. Work on the ground floor of the white marble bell tower began in 1173. The tower began to sink after construction had progressed to the second floor five years later. This was due to a mere three-meter foundation, set in weak, unstable subsoil, a design that was flawed from the beginning. Fortunately, builders have learned a few things since then.

When my wife and I built our home I discovered that leadership corresponds to the phases of home building. Constructing a house occurs in three major phases: foundation, framing and finish-out.

Building a team, like building a house, requires starting from the ground up. Our foundation, like our values, affects our team the same way all the time. When we lay our foundation, the homebuilder is committed to a certain floor planonce the foundation is set. This floorplan dictates how house will flow. **The team builder is committed to foundational values – how his team will flow and interact.**

I remember the first time I expressed my leadership values to my team. I called them "Lee's 3 F's": Focused, Fair and Fun. They formed the foundation for what I expected from my team and what they could expect from me.

Framing defines the parameters (systems and processes) within which each team member performs their job. Leadership framing consists of goal setting, training, decision-making processes, work procedures, problem solving – all the mechanisms used to get work done.

The finish-out adds the final, personal touch – it makes each house special and each relationship unique. Finish-out makes each person think that the house or team they built is their very own. As a result, they treat it with a sense of ownership vs. an "apartment job" they view as short term. Leadership finish-out comes in the form of building relationships and trust with our team by living our values, by walking our talk.

Regardless of how well-designed our framing and finish-out are, **our team's house can only be as strong as the leadership foundation we have built** … and our commitment to inspire excellence can only be as strong as our foundation.

Sometimes cracks in our foundational values are difficult to detect. Our tendency is to fix the problem at hand. We see a crack in the floor tile, so we replace the tile. A bedroom door doesn't swing quite right, so we adjust the hinges. A window doesn't close flush, so we caulk the bottom to seal the gap.

Cracks on our team's foundational values can initially look like a simple finish-out or framing problem. It's funny how we can find ourselves continually fixing the same framing and finish-out problems, but we do not realize these are symptoms of a deeper crack in our values. For instance, we might have several departments that are not keeping each other in the loop, so we restructure departments. This quick solution will not address the root cause of lack of mutual trust.

If we find ourselves dealing with the same issues repeatedly, we are probably not going deep enough with our solutions. What looks like an innocent crack in the wall (a small blip in employee turnover) could actually indicate a deeper crack in our foundation (team sees a disconnect between values and actions).

Inspiring leaders look beyond the symptoms to ensure that they are protecting team values. They know they must pour a strong foundation before they build a house to lead in.

Is my team clear about our team values?

_____

_____

_____

Does my team know my leadership values?

_____

_____

_____

What can I do to ensure my values guide my behavior and the behavior of my team?

_____

_____

_____

"Relativity applies to physics,
not ethics" (or values).

– ALBERT EINSTEIN

Vision

About 350 years ago, a shipload of travelers landed on the northeast coast of America. The first year, they established a town site. The next year, they elected a town government. The third year, the town government planned to build a road five miles westward into the wilderness. In the fourth year, the people tried to impeach their town government because they thought it was a waste of public funds to build a road five miles westward into a wilderness. Who needed to go there anyway?

These were people who had the vision to see 3,000 miles across an ocean and overcome great hardships to get there.

But in just a few years, they were not able to see even five miles out of town. They had lost their pioneering vision.

With a clear vision of what we can become, no ocean of difficulty is too great. Without it, we rarely move beyond our current boundaries.

Since most people have seen their share of visions from plenty of different leaders, set yourself apart by casting a high-definition vision. The challenge is that we tend to fall short of providing the level of clarity most people want and need so they can see the impact of their work. Leadership research supports this tendency toward a very low-definition vision. A groundbreaking Harris Poll found that:

- Only 15 percent of workers could identify their organization's most important goals.

- A majority of workers (51 percent) did not understand what they were supposed to do to help the organization achieve its goals.

- Less than half of available work time (49 percent) was spent on the organization's most important goals.

A clear vision answers these "Fundamental Four" questions being asked by your team, whether or not you hear them:

1. *What are we trying to achieve?* (Goals)

2. *How are we going to achieve it?* (Plans)

3. *How can I contribute?* (Roles)

4. *What's in it for me?* (Rewards)

The clarity of our answers to these questions is directly proportionate to the clarity of our vision. If you forget to answer any of these or just assume your team knows the answers, your vision will become a blur of disconnected mega pixels. You will have a team going in different directions or worse, not even wanting to venture a few steps into the forest.

A vision helps teams see where they are going and how they can help get there. People naturally feel more accountable for their performance when they clearly understand they are a part of something bigger than themselves.

Take a moment to cast a high-definition vision. It will inspire your team to venture to new and exciting destinations with you!

Can my team clearly and consistently state the vision for our team?

_____

_____

_____

Which of the "Fundamental Four" questions do I need to do a better job of answering for my team?

_____

_____

_____

"*Vision looks inward*
and becomes duty.
Vision looks outward
and becomes aspiration.
Vision looks upward
and becomes faith."

– STEPHEN S. WISE

Words

Some people literally change the world. People like Jesus, Gandhi, Albert Einstein, Mother Teresa, Ben Franklin and Steve Jobs.

Although it's an ambitious goal to change the world, we often underestimate our singular power to change the world of those around us. We don't have to be Oprah giving away free cars to positively change someone's world. **We each have that same power to change someone's world.** We don't even have to do anything! We only have to say three simple words.

Try one of these three-word, power-packed statements to change someone's world:

○ I thank you.

○ You are terrific.

○ I am sorry.

> ○ I trust you.

> ○ I promise you. (And keep it!)

> ○ I can help.

>> ○ I understand you.

>> ○ You are talented.

>> ○ You will succeed.

>>> ○ You inspire me.

>>> ○ I forgive you.

>>> ○ You're the best!

Whether we have a long conversation with a friend or simply place an order at a restaurant, every word makes a difference. **The results of our interactions are rarely neutral;** they are almost always positive or negative. Ask yourself, "Do my words reflect my commitment to help others, create win-wins, continuously learn, embrace change, and support my team's success?"

Words are the seeds of commitment. We plant the seeds with each movement of our lips. Once they are spoken, our words either grow in the form of an immediate response or they take time to germinate. Whether the result becomes apparent sooner or later, we cannot speak words of failure and defeat and expect a life of success and victory.

Use positive words to plant the seeds of success in team members' minds and hearts. You'll start a positive ripple effect in *their* world and in *the* world. Start with three simple words.

Who in my world needs to hear me say one of these phrases today?

_____

_____

_____

Which three words would I say?

_____

_____

_____

What difference do I think it would make if I spoke these words to them?

_____

_____

_____

"When words are scarce
    they are seldom spent in vain."

– WILLIAM SHAKESPEARE

No Matter What

Inspiring leadership is an inside job. You must lead yourself to a higher level before you can inspire extraordinary results from your team. You cannot lead where you dare not go.

In today's hyper-demanding business environment, there are plenty of reasons *not* to inspire personal excellence. A poor economy, a company restructuring or merger, B-list players on my team, more market competition, challenges at home with kids, and many, many more. It is often easier to point your finger at your team demanding excellence without living it first. However, inspiring leaders let their actions rise above their excuses. No excuses, no matter what.

Inspiring leaders turn stumbling blocks into stepping stones. First, take a step back and remain calm in the face of an apparent barrier. Second, reframe that barrier into an opportunity. Third, use gray matter to see the gray in the situation vs. seeing it as black and white. Considering all possibilities while staying calm predictably inspires new solutions that enable success. Look for alternatives and find solutions. Success is the only option, no matter what.

The personal example you set is the most inspiring leadership tool you have. Set an example of personal accountability and watch your team take more accountability. Keep a positive attitude in the face of adversity and watch your team do the same. Invest in your team's improvement and success and they will pass along that gift to the next generation of leaders. Live and work with unyielding integrity and watch your team values come to life. Lead with inspiration and watch your team perform inspired. Walk the talk, no matter what.

When you are pouring yourself into your team and not seeing immediate results, know that your investment is taking root and will soon inspire extraordinary results. So, if you are ever feeling discouraged or unappreciated, remember this: Leadership matters … no matter what!

"I attribute my success to this:
I never gave or took an excuse."

– FLORENCE NIGHTINGALE

Inspire Extraordinary Results!

The L Group, Inc. is a leadership and organizational development firm that provides practical consulting, high-impact training and inspiring products. We help you engage your team and execute your plans to achieve extraordinary results. Our services and resources address the three levels of leadership: Personal, Team and Organizational.

Virtually every *Fortune 500* company has experienced the positive impact of our practical approach, including:

Ambit Energy ○ AmeriSource Bergen Specialty Group ○ AutoTrader.com ○ AT&T Wireless ○ Crosstex Energy Services ○ CVS/Pharmacy ○ Dollar Tree Stores ○ Elbit Systems of America ○ Fossil ○ Foxworth-Galbraith Lumber Co. ○ International Paper ○ Jo-Ann Stores ○ Johnson Controls ○ KPMG ○ National Motor Club ○ Pegasus Solutions ○ Senior Living Properties ○ Pier 1 Imports ○ Texas Instruments ○ The Hartford ○ The Venetian Resort ○ TRANE ○ Verizon ○ Voluntary Hospitals of America ○ Yum! Brands

THE **L** GROUP
Leadership at every level.

Get inspired so you can inspire your team. Subscribe to a free, e-newsletter at theLgroup.com.

Leadership Matters

☑ YES! Please send me extra copies of *Leadership Matters*!

1-30 copies $16.95   31-100 copies $15.95   100+ copies $14.95

| *Leadership Matters* | ____ copies X _____ = $ _____ |

Other books by Lee J. Colan:

Sticking to It: The Art of Adherence	____ copies X $9.95	= $ _____
Passionate Performance	____ copies X $9.95	= $ _____
Orchestrating Attitude	____ copies X $9.95	= $ _____
Inspire!	____ copies X $9.95	= $ _____
Power Exchange	____ copies X $9.95	= $ _____
107 Ways to Stick to It	____ copies X $9.95	= $ _____
7 Moments…That Define Excellent Leaders	____ copies X $14.95	= $ _____
The Nature of Excellence (Classic Edition)	____ copies X $15.95	= $ _____
Engaging the Hearts and Minds of All Your Employees	____ copies X $21.95	= $ _____
Winners ALWAYS Quit	____ copies X $14.95	= $ _____

Shipping & Handling $ _____

Subtotal $ _____

Sales Tax (8.25%-TX Only) $ _____

Total (U.S. Dollars Only) $ _____

Shipping and Handling Charges

Total $ Amount	Up to $49	$50-$99	$100-$249	$250-$1199	$1200-$2999	$3000+
Charge	$7	$9	$16	$30	$80	$125

Name _____ Job Title _____

Organization _____ Phone _____

Shipping Address _____ Fax _____

Billing Address _____ Email _____
(Required for downloadable products)

City _____ State _____ ZIP _____

❑ Please invoice (Orders over $200) Purchase Order Number (if applicable) _____

Charge Your Order: ❑ MasterCard   ❑ Visa   ❑ American Express

Credit Card Number _____ Exp. Date _____

Signature _____

❑ Check Enclosed (Payable to: CornerStone Leadership)

Fax: 972.274.2884   **Mail: P.O. Box 764087**
Dallas, TX 75376   **Phone: 888.789.5323**

Thank you for reading *Leadership Matters!*

We hope it has assisted you in your quest for
personal and professional growth.
CornerStone Leadership is committed to
providing new and enlightening products
to organizations worldwide.

Our mission is to fuel knowledge with
practical resources that will accelerate
your team's productivity, success and job satisfaction!

Best wishes for your continued success.

CornerStone
Leadership Institute

www.CornerStoneLeadership.com

*Start a crusade in your organization –
have the courage to learn, the vision to lead,
and the passion to share.*